F.T. DAWSON

PRACTICAL INTELLIGENCE

The Ultimate Guide on How to Master Your Mind, Discover How Mentalism Can Help You How to Live a Free and More Fulfilling Life

Descrierea CIP a Bibliotecii Naționale a României
F.T. DAWSON
    PRACTICAL INTELLIGENCE. The Ultimate Guide on How to Master Your Mind, Discover How Mentalism Can Help You How to Live a Free and More Fulfilling Life / F.T. Dawson –
Bucharest: Editura My Ebook, 2021
    ISBN

F.T. DAWSON

PRACTICAL INTELLIGENCE

The Ultimate Guide on How to Master Your Mind, Discover How Mentalism Can Help You How to Live a Free and More Fulfilling Life

My Ebook Publishing House
Bucharest, 2021

TABLE OF CONTENTS

INTRODUCTION

The famous French Enlightenment philosopher Jean-Jacques Rousseau famously said "Man was born free. But everywhere, he is in chains."

Of course, Rousseau was talking about politics and religious systems when he said this. However, his observation is spot-on regarding how most people choose to live their lives. We are born free, but we choose to walk around in chains. It doesn't matter that the chains are invisible; their effects are still noticeable.

Let that sink in. People are born free because they have tremendous power over their reality. But when you look at the way most people live their lives, it's as if they are slaves. They have all these imaginary lines that they have drawn for themselves. Things like who they can and cannot be, what they are and what they're not, where they can go and what's off-limits.

Believe it or not all of us actively shape our reality. Our minds make us the masters of our reality. The fact that you're taking this training with a certain attitude and you were able to buy this training in the first place means you are a master of your reality.

It doesn't matter whether you accept that or not. It doesn't matter whether you are aware of this or not. It's still the reality. In fact, just through the daily operations of your mind, you master and edit your reality.

What's the problem? Well, most of us don't claim this power. We live our lives based on obligation. That's right. We try to be the kind of people our parents expect us to be. We try to live our lives based on other people's expectations.

We also get used to certain customs. Maybe it's part of our culture. Perhaps it's part of our little group. Whatever the case may be, unless we choose to open our eyes, we do things the same way as the people we hang out with. Birds of a feather flock together indeed.

We also turn our backs on our tremendous mental power to shape our reality by sticking close to tradition. Just because something has been done the same way hundreds of years doesn't necessarily mean that you should do the same. Just because there is such a thing as conventional wisdom doesn't mean that it's the only type of wisdom applicable to you.

Finally, you're walking around wearing your invisible chains because of bad mental and physical habits. It seems like no matter hard you try to change things or turn things around; your habits keep pulling you back. It's as if you only need to see or feel certain things, and you start acting in an almost automatic way. It is very discouraging. It makes you feel weak, small, and insignificant.

Mentalism teaches you to refocus your energy so that instead of these mental processes working against you, you train your mind to make it work for you. You only need to look at very successful people to see how this works. You only need to talk to very happy people and realize that they're operating from a totally different place. You can achieve the same.

This training steps you through the process of how mentalism can help you live a more fulfilling life.

CHAPTER 1

PEEL BACK THE CURTAINS AND YOU'LL SEE

THE REALITY OF YOUR LIFE

I don't want to mix metaphors here but just like people can easily live their lives wearing invisible shackles, we can also live our lives completely surrounded by invisible curtains. When you put curtains in your house, you do it to block out light. It's your way of regulating natural lighting that comes through your windows.

Did you know that you're doing the same with reality? However, instead of windows, you have your mind, and there are certain beliefs and practices that we have that block out reality. At the very least, it prevents us from seeing things as they really are.

Most people are mentally lazy. There, I said it. We really are.

First of all, the older you get, the more you assume things. Now, I can't blame you for thinking this way because when you were growing up, you had to experience things first hand and then make predictions based on those experiences or based on what people tell you about those experiences. You have to go through that process so you can learn enough to see certain patterns.

As you get older, you can safely rely on the wealth of experience you've had and more or less make certain assumptions. At this point, you would think that it is fairly safe for you to assume that once you see certain patterns, then you pretty much can see the rest of what will happen.

This makes a lot of sense in most situations. You don't want to sit around and wait for things to fully develop when you know full well there's a high chance that things will turn out the way they've always turned out. However, this can only go so far.

Also, when you get older, you tend to use this power of assumption in situations where they don't count or at least they shouldn't be applied to. You can use this with people you meet, and this can lead to very unfair and even downright cruel dismissal of people.

I remember one time I was at a business meeting and one of the guys who was supposed to make a presentation showed up in shorts and flip-flops. At the back of my mind, I automatically assumed that this person was a slacker. No way is this guy serious.

He made his presentation and he left. I only learned a week later that person was actually a multi-billionaire. So much for my assumptions, right? It turned out that we needed him more than he needed us. He obviously did not need our money.

I assumed that since he had that attire or lack thereof that he wasn't professional or that he was some sort of loser. Do you see how this works? As you get older, you need less and less input for you to jump to conclusions, and this can be very dangerous. You might actually be locking yourself out from a tremendous amount of truths and opportunities out there.

Another form of mental laziness involves your expectations. In a way, this works in a similar way to assumptions. When we find ourselves in certain situations, we think we are right to expect certain results. We feel that somehow some way we're entitled to certain things.

This is a problem because the more entitled you feel to certain results, the less likely you are to work for them. You're less likely to be open-minded.

You're not looking for a challenge. You become less flexible. It can lead to a serious mess.

Unfortunately, the only person we have to blame is ourselves. It's too easy to become a prisoner of one's expectations.

Finally, we can develop such a crippling sense of entitlement that we do not take initiative. We feel that the world has to come to us. We feel that people have to impress us, or they have to take the first step or make the effort.

I'm sorry to be the one to break this to you but if you're trying to make it in this world, you're going to have to take the initiative.

You're going to have to bring value to other people's lives. It's not like they owe you fame, riches and power. You have to prove yourself. You have to establish a track record. You have to develop a brand. All of these take initiative.

All the things that I've described above can act like mental curtains. In fact, the longer you refuse to cast aside those curtains, the easier it would be for you to feel stuck. Please understand that you're feeling mentally stuck not because somebody has a gun pointed at your head and demands that you be miserable and powerless.

Instead, you have allowed this mental laziness and all these negative mental habits to get the better of you so you basically end up focusing on the tried and proven, the known quantities or the safe spaces in your life.

Everything else is off-limits. You just can't be bothered with them. You'd rather focus on what you think you "know".

This is mental laziness. These act as curtains that block out the healthy challenges you need to master reality. To peel back the curtains of your life, you need to do one thing: take inventory of your life.

Have you ever worked for a retail store? When I worked for a pharmacy right after high school, I was hired as temporary staff to take inventory. I didn't know that the typical drugstore had so much stuff. I saw this firsthand because I had to count everything.

That's what an inventory is. You have a clipboard in one hand and you have a pen in the other, and you are looking through different categories and subcategories of products, physically counting these products, sorting them. Sometimes we have to take out a box and store stuff away.

In many cases, we have to go to back storage room, take stuff out of boxes, count them as well as count and mark the boxes. That's a lot of counting, that's a lot of tracking and a lot of monitoring. That's how an inventory works.

You have to do the same with your life. You have to take inventory of your life. Believe it or not, this is more difficult because instead of counting stuff like medication bottles, product packages or envelopes and boxes, you're going to have to take inventory of the things that you assume to be true, what you expect from certain situations in your life.

You have to become aware of the situations where you adopt certain mindsets, and you have to pay attention to your lack of initiative.

That's a lot of stuff. This requires heavy mental lifting. It also requires a tremendous amount of honesty. Let's face it. Do you feel good when somebody says that you're lazy? Do you get butterflies in your stomach when somebody says in so many ways that you are living a lie? Of course not.

Most people don't want to hear that kind of stuff, but that's exactly the kind of conclusion that you would get if you take an honest inventory of your life. It would turn out, and I can guarantee this, that a lot of the things that you assumed to be a certain way in your life are actually quite different. They turn out to be very different from what you assume them to be.

They may be familiar. You might not even consciously think about them, but once you start peeling back your mental curtains and you start putting in the work to see things for what they are, you might be in for a rude shock.

CHAPTER 2

OUR LIVES ARE INTENTIONAL

You may be thinking that the title of this chapter is pretty non-controversial. You may be forgiven for thinking that. Most people would agree with this. I beg to differ. Seriously.

How come? Well, if you say to somebody who is down on his luck and who is struggling, to put food on the table that his life is in intentional and that somehow some way he chose that life, you might not get a happy response. In fact, you might even get punched in the face.

How dare you say something like that? Would anybody who's struggling, who is facing all sorts of issues like health problems, legal problems, divorce and mental issues intend that kind of life? Would they really choose that kind of life? Talk about insulting.

Don't be surprised if you get this kind of reaction. However, regardless of how people react to this reality, it is still reality. I know it's a hard pill to swallow.

You have to remember that once a person makes a certain decision and the consequences of that decision appear, that person becomes very, very creative in making up all sorts of excuses, justifications and reasons to blame others for what happened. We all have that inner genius in us.

However, none of this, as painful and unpleasant as it may be on many levels, takes away from the fact that our lives are intentional. How come? Our internal world is the cause of our external world. That's right.

Everything about you that other people can observe ultimately came from your internal mental processes. This can be something as shallow and superficial as your haircut, what kind of clothes you wear, how much you weigh, your complexion, how healthy your skin is.

This also explains how big your house is or whether you're renting or owning. This is also the cause of the kind of car or means of transportation you have.

Your internal world also explains how much money you have in the bank, how much respect people give you, the kind of degrees you have or don't have, so on and so forth.

All these come from within. This is a very, very touchy issue for a lot of people because once we all agree that our lives are intentional because of our internal world producing our external result, it becomes obvious that somewhere down the line, some people made the wrong choice.

People don't like to be wrong. People don't like to be made to feel that they're being blamed for their own failures or bad decisions. That's just part of human nature. It's to be expected. It's definitely a big blow to the ego.

However, regardless of how much it hurts, nothing can take away from the fact that everything people can see from outside of you is a product of your internal choices. To get that car, you had to make a choice. To get that job, which produces a certain income which affords you a certain lifestyle, you had to make a choice or a series of choices.

To get that degree or to drop out of high school, you had to make certain choices. All these are internal and guess what? They can be traced to your values.

These values are not set by heaven for you. They're not inherited from somebody else. They're not something that just dropped into your lap. They're choices. Just as some people can choose certain values which lead to a certain lifestyle and certain life results, others can choose other values which produce different results.

Again, this is not welcome news to a lot of people. People do not like to be confronted face to face with this reality.

Everything in Our Lives are Choices

Don't get me wrong. Sometimes your responses to whatever the world brings your way are repeated so frequently that they seem almost automatic. Don't assume that just because you can predictably respond a certain way when you detect certain things that this is somehow automatic behavior. Don't fool yourself into thinking that you have absolutely no choice when you take certain actions.

No. All these habits actually spring from choices. It takes a while to develop a new habit. In fact, according to some estimates, picking up a new habit or breaking one can take anywhere from twenty-one days to sixty days. You have to repeat the same pattern before you develop or break a habit.

What are you doing prior to that point? That's right. You're choosing to take those actions. These are choices.

Since you're making choices all the time to produce certain results and consequences, your life is intentional. You may not accept it. It may be uncomfortable. It definitely is not a convenient truth, but it is still the truth. Embrace this fact.

Instead of living your life on autopilot, wrap your arms around the concept of intentionality. Master your life or author your life by being as intentional as you can about what you choose to think. This is the bedrock of mentalism.

That's how you edit your reality. That's how you go from thinking about a certain outcome to actually seeing, hearing, touching, tasting and smelling that outcome. In other words, you turn ideas into reality. You're not just hoping and wishing. You're not just thinking "it would be nice" if certain things existed. You're actually taking action.

CHAPTER 3

TOO MANY OF US CHOOSE TO BE BLIND

Who in their right mind would consciously blind themselves? I can't even think of one person who would do that. You have a serious competitive advantage when you can see. Even if you can see with just one eye, you still have a massive advantage over somebody who has no sight at all.

Interestingly enough, a lot of people choose to be blind at some level or other. I'm not talking about being physically or legally blind. I'm talking about overlooking a very important power that they have. You have to understand that in any group of people, 20% will always make more money, have more sex, achieve better results, own more stuff, you name it.

Regardless of how you measure success, these 20% will always come out on top. This, after all, is the Pareto principle. How bad is this inequality? Well, you only need to look at the fact that a tiny fraction of the world's population owns most of the wealth. They didn't steal it all. They didn't point a gun at people's heads and force them to give it up. They earned it.

Unfortunately, the vast majority of people are left struggling over the leftovers. Most people are content with fighting over the crumbs that are left over by the 20%. These 20% or less are fully aware of their power. They are not blind to their human superpower. What am I talking about? Although our lives are the result of our choices, we choose to be blind to this truth.

It may seem banal. It might even seem like common sense, but the moment you truly believe that your life is the result of your choices, you would start thinking, talking, and acting a different way. Whatever it is that's frustrating you will sooner or later go away. That's how important choices are. Sadly, a lot of people choose to be blind about this.

They do things on autopilot. They do not make conscious decisions. It's like they're going through the motions of life. Now, it's easy to understand this intellectually. It's even tempting to say, "I don't do that," or "I'm going to stop doing that." Congratulations, at least you're making some progress. But here's the problem. This is built into the human condition.

That's right. This is part of human nature. At the end of the day, there are two fundamental truths about human beings. First of all, we are very scared of change. We can talk a good game about how we welcome change and how important innovation and disruption are to us, but at the end of the day, we grow accustomed to doing things a certain way. Our actions fall into a certain pattern.

The other fundamental truth about human beings, regardless of where they come from and what they look like, is that we tend to take the path of least resistance. Let's put it this way. If somebody offered you a plateful of yummy German chocolate cake or you can dig a hole for two hours straight, which would you rather pick? It doesn't take a rocket scientist to figure this out.

We take the path of least resistance which means that we run away from pain, discomfort or inconvenience and we run towards pleasure, convenience and expediency. Given these two truths about the human condition, it's easy to see why people end up doing things on autopilot. They end up making decisions in a certain way.

It doesn't matter where they are or what time it is. They end up doing the exact same things. As you already know, our lives are the results of our choices, so we end up feeling stuck. We end up denying the fact that we can choose. It must be something else. It can't be the fact that I chose my life. No, that's not it. That's too much to take. No way.

This is the internal monologue most people play with themselves. That's why they remain blind to their human superpower. Your human superpower is your ability to choose. I know it's easy to say. It kind of rolls off the tongue.

Most people can intellectually accept that, but they don't really accept it. It's kind of like something that we all agree on, but we then quickly discount it.

You will always have a choice. At the very least, you can choose how you respond to the things happening around you. As I vividly explained in the previous chapter regarding the example of the burning building, choices can be made and undone. Wrap your mind around this. Stop choosing to be blind.

CHAPTER 4

THE CORE OF MENTALISM

How can Mentalism help you? How can this concept with a funny name enable you to live the life you've always wanted to live? Well, as the term implies, Mentalism is all about your mind.

Believe it or not, your mind is extremely powerful. It is the metaphysical product of the physical actions of your brain. It exists above and beyond your brain. Don't think this is just a physical thing.

Don't think that your mind is just a byproduct of your brain's physical processes. It's more than that. Mentalism is all about helping people understand how their thoughts impact their lives. With that understanding in place, Mentalism helps people live the lives they want by teaching them to change the only thing they can fully control in this universe.

Let me be clear: there is one thing that you can fully control-your mind. Mentalism helps you live the life that you have always wanted to live by helping you fully control your thoughts. Change your thoughts and you change your life.

Viewed from this perspective, Mentalism is all about taking control of your life. If you are in any way unhappy, frustrated or feeling stuck in any area of your life, Mentalism can help you make important changes.

Mentalism can help you become more content, fulfilled and yes, happy. But none of this will be possible if you don't let Mentalism help you achieve one thing that you obviously are struggling with. Again, if you're taking this training, it means that at least one part of your life isn't exactly a bed of roses. Maybe you have many areas of your life that you are struggling with.

Still, for Mentalism to help you, you have to be willing to take ownership of your life. This is crucial. This means you have to let go of blaming other people or circumstances beyond your control for whatever you're struggling with. This also means moving on from the past. I understand that you may have had a difficult past.

Maybe you are a survivor of abuse. Maybe you made bad decisions in the past and you're feeling guilty about them. Maybe there are certain people around you that create a hostile or toxic environment that really eats away at your self-esteem and motivation.

Taking ownership means letting go of all of that and focusing instead on what you can control. Ultimately, when all the dust has settled in our lives, there is really only one thing we control and that is our thoughts. This is Mentalism's bedrock principle: control your thoughts and you control your life.

How Mentalism works

Mentalism is actually made up of five different beliefs. You have to believe in these principles, otherwise it's not going to work for you. Here they are in short order.

Principle #1 All stimuli are neutral
Principle #2 Change your mental filters
Principle #3 Change your mental habits
Principle #4 Change your emotional response habits
Principle #5 Change your reality through changed actions

All of these flow into each other and are dependent on each other. For Mentalism to create the kind of change you have been dreaming of in your life, you have to believe in all these principles and let them work in your life. This is crucial because if you don't believe any of these principles, then Mentalism is not going to work for you. After all, it's all about thought ownership.

Unfortunately, if you disavow this process, it would be very hard for you to take ownership of your thoughts because in the back of your mind, you believe that it doesn't work, that you're wasting your time or this just a bunch of hocus pocus. This leads me to a very important point that can undermine the effectiveness of Mentalism.

CHAPTER 5

ALL STIMULI ARE NEUTRAL

Believe it or not, the world is neutral. I know it's kind of hard to believe. After all, it seems that your boss has it in for you. It seems that people just don't get you, so they say and do all sorts of negative things.

Sometimes you wake up on the wrong side of the bed and it seems like the whole world has turned against you. But if you're completely honest and you look at the big picture of what's going on and you dare to process everything past your emotions, there is only one conclusion: the world is neutral.

It may not seem like it, but it is. Here's how it works. Every single moment, you are picking up thousands of signals. These signals are things that you see, hear, touch, taste and smell. In other words, you're using your five senses to pick up all this data from the world. This happens every single second. Now, let me ask you, are you fully aware of all those signals that you are picking up?

Of course not. Your mind is only zeroing in on a tiny fraction of the data you could possibly pay attention to. It's as if you're looking at the night sky and you zoom in on a corner. That's how your mind works. This is called perception.

This is all a choice. It may seem habitual because it may very well have turned into a habit, but it started off as a choice.

Different people with different mindsets, attitudes and belief systems choose to pick up on different things depending on their experiences and their background.

For instance, if you grew up in a rough neighborhood and you find yourself walking down the street in an otherwise safe neighborhood, I can guarantee you that you are still picking up stimuli from the outside world the same way you did in your old neighborhood.

When you compare notes with people who grew up in that safe neighborhood, they probably would be paying attention to other things. Your main focus is security and survival. Do you see how this works?

We're just talking about perception here. We're not even talking about giving these perceived stimuli meaning, which is the next step.

You give your stimuli meaning

When you choose to focus on a certain se t of stimuli, you give meaning to these facts. Not only did you choose what you became aware of, you also choose the meaning of these facts. Again, two totally different people from different walks of life can have two totally different interpretations of basically the same set of stimuli.

This is a choice. It's interesting enough that you choose what set of data to focus on and then you take it to the next level by interpreting the data in your own way, which is definitely different from the way the next person analyzes the same set of data. This is your mindset. This is your attitude. This is your perspective. Understand that you own these things.

These were not pumped into your brain. People did not force you to think this way. Somewhere down the line, you chose to think this way. Again, it may seem like a habit. It may even seem like it's just part of your personality because you repeatedly do this, but it all started out as a choice.

I need you to keep coming back to that point. If you believe that you have a choice, then you have power over your life. Just as you can choose to do certain things, you can choose to stop doing them and do something else.

You choose what you think about

Now that you have given these stimuli meaning, then you start thinking about them. What do they mean? How do they impact you? Most importantly, how do they relate to your personal narrative? Please remember that people always carry around a personal movie script. I'm not talking about a physical manuscript that they lug from point A to point B. I'm talking about their personal story that they keep reciting in their heads.

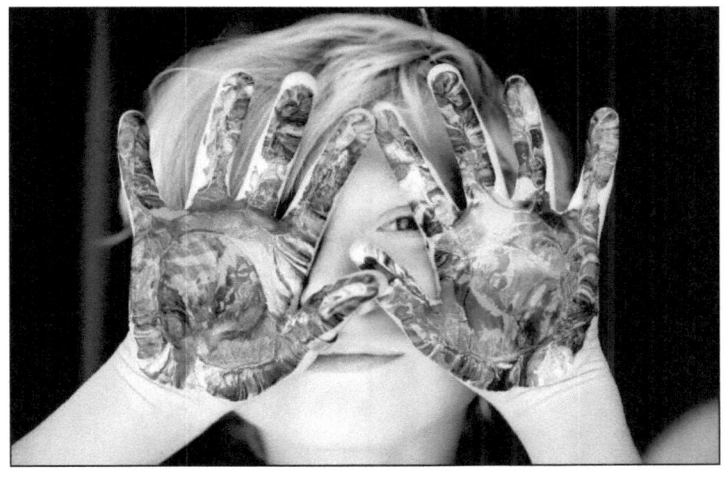

They keep saying, "This is who I am. This is who I'm not. This is what happened to me. This is what I'm capable of. This is where I'm going. This is what I've done," so on and so forth. This is your personal script. Everybody has one. It's called your identity. When you break down that identity, there is a narrative and then there is a script.

When you choose to become aware of certain things instead of other things and you choose to give them one set of meanings instead of another, you plug in what you choose to remember about that particular experience to your script. I hope it's abundantly clear that when you look at all these things that are happening, that you are always in control.

You choose what you become aware of. You choose the meaning that you give to the stimuli that you have chosen to become aware of. You choose what you think about. That's a lot of choices. I know it seems daunting, especially if you feel that you have no choice. It is quite frustrating to realize this given the fact that you feel like you're stuck in some sort of bad movie called your life.

I just want you to keep focusing on these different choice points to highlight the fact that you always have a choice. This was true in the past. This is true today. This will continue to be true in the future. You always have a choice. This is why I can safely say the next (shocking) conclusion: you are always in control.

Everything about you, what you habitually think about, what you talk about and, most importantly, what you choose you do, flow from your choice of thoughts. They all flow from your mindset. They all flow from the mental filter you chose to install.

This is control. I know this is not a very popular answer. It would be great if happiness can come in some sort of capsule or enlightenment can be packaged in some sort of tablet, but this is the way it is.

The world is neutral. It's your mind that gives it shape and color. Always come back to this reality. Once you have fully accepted this, everything becomes so much easier. The other four principles of Mentalism flow from this fact. Accept that the world's stimuli are neutral. If you're able to truly believe that, then progress is possible. If you can't, then you're going to be stuck.

You're always going to come back to the negative mindsets that you have regarding you being some sort of victim. You have to believe that all stimuli are neutral. Without this fundamental belief, no progress is possible with Mentalism.

CHAPTER 6

CHANGE YOUR MENTAL FILTER

This chapter describes a very momentous step in practicing mentalism. As difficult as it may be for a lot of people, accepting the fact that the world and its stimuli are essentially neutral is actually the easiest part. It's absolutely necessary and no progress can be made if you can't make it past that point but, in the big scheme of things, that part is the easiest.

Everything else past that point requires a tremendous amount of effort. Now I'm not saying that you're going to have to roll up your sleeves and break out in a sweat. This is not a physical effort. Instead, this is something much more difficult.

Believe it or not, it's easier for people to do things physically than for them to take action mentally. When you take a mental action, you're going to be facing more resistance. Why? You're going to be going against how you normally think. You're going to have to confront and overcome your mental habits.

You're going to have to deal with your attitude. This is why changing your mental filter is so difficult for a lot of people. As the old saying goes you can take the kid out of the country, but you cannot take the country out of the kid.

Now you can mix and match all sorts of things for the word kid and country, but you get to decide whether you will get the same result. We are a product of our upbringing, our environment, and our past. These work together with our choices to produce our mental filter. Please understand given this reality it's very hard to change your mental filter.

How Does Your Mental Filter Affect Your Life?

It all boils down to interpretation. Since the stimuli coming in are essentially neutral and we choose to become aware of certain facts instead of others this leads to short interpretations. These certain facts are more likely to support certain interpretations. If that isn't bad enough we then look at what we choose to pay attention to and pick one of many different interpretations.

Now you may be thinking at this point. It's fairly straightforward. No, it isn't. This isn't just happening in your mind. It isn't just something that is easy to blow off where we can easily say well everybody looks at different things in different ways and it all leads to the same place anyways. No, it doesn't.

Because you chose to interpret what you choose to pay attention to as a certain way.

This leads to emotional states. Please understand that interpretations are never emotionally neutral. There's always an emotional payload to them. It may not involve drama. It may not involve some sort of strong emotion but there is still an emotional component.

Believe it or not, not caring or apathy is an emotional state. Now that your interpretation has triggered this emotional state what happens next while your emotional state like it or not and regardless of whether you are aware of it impacts how you talk and act.

It also impacts what you focus on. When you start talking a certain way with people you start influencing people around you because they listen to you. More importantly, when you act a certain way because you assume that things are a certain way. These actions are not restricted to you. This is the point where your thoughts change your reality. Let's get one thing clear.

The world doesn't care about your feelings. It really doesn't. It couldn't care less about your motivations intentions ideas theories and whatnot. If you just keep them in your head. Even if you express them very emotionally. Chances are the world still wouldn't care.

Now there's a good chance that you would have a strong impact if you actually published this information. And it caught a lot of people's attention. Still, by and large, your intentions and emotions really don't impact the world. However, the world cannot help but sit up and pay attention.

When you let your emotional state change how you behave at that point you start changing your reality, at that point, your actions start impacting the people and the things around you. You start changing your world and the world can't help but react. This is how we edit our reality.

And it all begins with our thoughts and mental filters. By just making key changes at each step of the process you end up changing the actions you take. When you change your habitual actions, you change your life. This is how mentalism works. It's all about taking full ownership of your mental filter.

Choosing an Empowering Filter

When you read certain situations in your life whether they're happening now or whether it happened in the past. Always understand that you can choose your filter. Always understand that there is at least one filter that is empowering. At the very least it won't make you feel small weak powerless and passive. Find that filter. Read a situation in a way where you remain in control.

You will always say to yourself if I feel negative it is because I've chosen to feel negative. If I feel small and weak and powerless it's because I've chosen to feel that way. And the more you keep coming back to that affirmative statement of a quote. It's because I have chosen that quote. You are doing it right. You are on the right path. Why? Because you have chosen to take off your blinders to the superpower you have.

The only power you need in this life is your choice. Your power of choice. This is what shapes your reality. This is what gives birth to a brand new or universal universe of opportunities for yourself. You are not your past even if you're 50 years old. You can still go back to school. You can get retrained even if you have been physically abused bruised and battered in the past.

You can still have better relationships. It's your choice. And all of this it is all your choice. This is why you have to keep coming back to the power of your choice. This is the most empowering realization you'll ever get. Use this as the bedrock of all filters. You choose to be aware of, and you choose to craft for yourself.

CHAPTER 7

CHANGE YOUR MENTAL HABITS

I know in Chapter 6 we did quite a bit of heavy lifting. Believe me.

Personally speaking, it's really very hard to process all the information in Chapter 6. Still, it's absolutely necessary. Now, if you thought Chapter 6 was difficult, Chapter 7 can be quite a doozy. How come? Well. It's one thing to realize the importance of our mental filters and how big of an impact they have on how we think, talk, feel and act.

Taking control over the whole process. It can be very, very challenging. This is due to the fact that as we get older we feel that there is really only one way we can behave. There's only one way we can respond to the world. Of course, as I've mentioned previously this is an illusion. You always have a choice.

In fact, if you draw the process out starting with your thoughts or starting with your perceptions all the way to your actions there are many specific and distinct points where you can step in and take control of the situation. Your choices in these distinct parts can drastically change the outcome of your situation.

That's right regardless of how seemingly hopeless, bleak and negative these previous parts maybe. You can still end up with a happy ending. The problem is it's easier to accept this intellectually than to process this on an emotional level.

They always say even the very best ideas that make intellectual sense to you are not going to help you in your practical everyday life unless they sink to the level of your heart. Although people hate to admit it when we're all emotional creatures.

I know this is especially true in the United States where "logic and rationality" are supposed to be top values. But the truth is according to a recent study, most people make decisions impulsively. That's right. They let their emotions get the better of them when it comes to their choices whether it's purchasing a product picking a girlfriend picking a school picking a course going on a job interview.

You name it. We often do things impulsively. Now what's interesting about the study is that when people were asked to explain their choices people gave all the participants time to study the subjects. They gave all sorts of seemingly logical and rational reasons why they came to the conclusions they did.

In other words, they first made the decision on impulse. And when they found the reason, they bring this up because this highlights the power of 'automatic thinking'.

You think those people who made those impulsive decisions were clearly mapping out their logic theory and the different probabilities of certain outcomes taking place based on their decision? Of course not. That's not how most people decide. Instead, they let their feelings get the better of them and this leads to habitual responses. In other words, they made decisions based on their mental habits.

If you want to practice mentalism and let it truly take your life to the next level. You have to change your mental habits. In fact, it's actually quite simple: change your habits and you change your life. It doesn't get any more basic than that. Now keep in mind that this works both ways. You can change your life for the worse or for the better. Still, the basic mechanism remains the same. It's all about changing your mental habits.

How Do Your Mental Habits Work?

Well as I mentioned in a previous chapter we perceive our reality and the world's stimuli as neutral, but our mental filters focus on only one set of data. And we interpret this data a certain way. This then leads to emotional states which trigger certain things we say, feel and do.

When we do certain things, we change our world. That is how our habits work. So, when we have a habitual way of picking up certain things from the outside world and this triggers a predictable chain of action, we can't help it. In fact, when you call people out on this one of the first things they will tell you is they can't help but this is who I am. No, it's not. It's not your identity.

This is not hard-coded in who you are. This is not hardwired into your intrinsic identity as a person, as a human being. This can be changed. This is again all a part of a series of choices. The fact that we choose to be with the fact that we choose to ignore these decision points doesn't make them go away. There are still choices.

The fact that this process seems to go by so quickly or even in an instant shows you the power of mental habits. If you want to change your life you have to change your mental habits. The first way to do this is to deconstruct how habits work perhaps.

Habits Deconstructed

'So, what' is a habitual action. Now don't get excited.

Again, it's a predictable or almost automatic action. Now don't get excited about action. This actually means more than physical actions. It can also involve mental processes and incites emotional states. They're not just physical habits but they're also mental habits. Now with that said the habit process is broken down into three parts.

There's the trigger, the habitual action, and the reward. For example, people who smoke. People who have a smoking habit are actually triggered to whip out a cancer stick and when they smoke they're actually seeking a reward.

For example, a lot of smokers habitually light up after a heavy meal. The fact that they just had a meal acts as a trigger.

And when they take the action of smoking cigarettes the rush created by the nicotine in their bloodstream due to a blood vessel constriction leads to a mental rush. Smokers interpret this mental rush as something positive. It is their reward. This physical reality brought about by hypertension is what they're shooting for. See how this works in IT and it plays out very quickly.

The moment you had a big meal and you were a smoker you get this insane urge to light up. How come? Well, you detected the trigger at the back of your mind you're thinking of that nice rush that you get after you smoke. It's a great after meal experience.

So, you light up and you get the reward and the more you repeat this the more the reward is associated with the trigger. In fact, it becomes so associated that you don't even think about it. You just need to be aware of that trigger.

The same applies to our thoughts. Our mental habits require thoughts or mental pictures and when we take habitual action on these thoughts which often takes the form of mental interpretation or emotional responses we get a reward. The reward is always the same reward. It isn't an emotional state.

For instance, if you remember an ex-boyfriend who used to slap you around or beat you the habitual mental action that many people would get is to say I am so happy that that person is no longer in my life.

And you get an emotional state of relief because you are with somebody else now. It doesn't occur to you that that exact same pattern might still be present in your current relationship. Instead, you just focus on the relief that this person whom you used to meet and who used to give you a black eye and treat you like garbage is out of your life. The reward is the sense of relief of moving on.

This is how mental habits work.

The key question is do your mental habits work for you instead of against you. You have to ask this key question if you want to change your mental habits. It's going to be very hard to get people to make important changes in their lives. If we all focus on the WHAT and the HOW. We also have to focus on the WHY. And the way to do this is to ask yourself do my mental habits work for me.

Do they improve my life? Do they enable me to live the kind of life I want for myself today? Do they make me happier or make me feel fulfilled, complete and satisfied? If not, then we have to make our habits work for us. This is where you lose a lot of people. Because it's easy to follow up to this point but a lot of people simply do not believe.

If you truly believe that you can choose your thoughts, then this should be fairly straightforward. You can make your mental habits work for you.

Before we get to the good news the bad news is you really cannot change your triggers and your rewards. The trigger of the past boyfriend who is very abusive. You really can't change that. It's going to happen.

Those mental images will flash because that person was in your life at some point in the past. Unless, of course, you get hit on the head and you develop amnesia. Those memories are not going to go away. This is a reality you cannot escape. That person was in your life. Get over it. Accept that. So that trigger is not going to go away.

The same applies to you. What's required here is a sense of relief that you are with somebody new or you have moved on. Own the fact that the triggers and the rewards are going to be the same. Now, what's missing? Well, your mental habitual action.

The point here is to come up with a different reaction to the mental trigger while claiming the same reward. Believe it or not, there are other ways you can get a nice buzz instead of smoking a cigarette. For example, if your trigger is you wake up in the morning and your normal instinct may be to light up.

Well, what if you swap lighting up with going for a walk or better yet a nice jog around the block?

You still get to the same result which is a nice buzz. But this time the buzz that you get is caused by endorphins instead of nicotine. However, since you've changed your physical habit of running instead of smoking you get other side benefits. You lose weight. You look better.

You pump more oxygen into your brain so your willpower is improved and your mental focus is enhanced. The whole nine yards and all it took is to change your habitual action that triggers the same and so is the reward.

Understand how this works because you have to do the same when it comes to your mental habits.

CHAPTER 8

CHANGE YOUR EMOTIONAL RESPONSE HABITS

This is probably the hardest part of Mentalism. You have to understand that whenever human emotions get thrown into the mix, all bets are off. Seriously.

As I have mentioned in a previous chapter, people make up all sorts of rational-sounding justifications for the decisions they originally made out of impulse. Imagine that. People make a decision due to some sort of emotional trigger, but when asked about it, they come up with something reasonable- sounding.

Well, that's how a lot of people deal with emotions. Most people don't want to admit it, but we all have a trigger. And once we get emotionally triggered, we end up responding in a very predictable way.

It's not unusual for people to think that this is just part of who they are. It's too easy to just chalk it all up to our personalities. But it's not really all that complicated.

What Could Go Wrong?

Well, if you let your emotions get the better of you, it's easy to fly off the handle, say things that you will eventually regret, or worse yet, do something that will harm your relationships, harm yourself, or land you in legal hot water. You can open a can of worms when you choose to let your emotions get the better of you as far as your actions go.

Pick Better Emotional Responses

As I've mentioned earlier in this training, you can change how you respond to triggers. This is crucial to Mentalism.

You don't have to fly off the handle. You don't have to break down and cry. You don't have to think it's the end of the world. You don't have to feel small, weak and powerless. There are other emotional responses out there. Given the context, they might be way better.

The best way to do this is to be intentional about it. Ask yourself, what state of mind am I looking for when it comes to my emotional responses? In other words, focus on the outcome instead of getting all caught up in the process.

Here are just some common positive emotional responses to triggers:

A Sense of Being in Control

Instead of getting angry and then letting that anger produce a negative chain reaction with the person or people you're upset at, why not focus on getting the trigger to yield a sense of being in control?

This is a very empowering feeling. Believe me, there's nothing more positive than finding yourself in the middle of a crowd where everybody seems to have lost their head and you're the only person level-headed enough to see the big picture.

The likelihood of positive outcomes in that particular setting is much higher than if you allowed yourself to get all caught up in the negative emotional state of everybody else. Also, when you get the sense that you are in control, you are able to see the big picture and identify options that a lot of people too often overlook or dismiss.

A Sense of Possibility

Another way you can emotionally respond to triggers is with a sense of possibility. Instead of automatically feeling that things are hopeless, that there's not much you can do, that you've seen this before and it all leads to heartbreak, failure and depression, try a sense of possibility.

In other words, instead of seeing the door close, look really hard and see what kind of doors and windows the situation opens. This is not always obvious, but when you focus on achieving the emotional response of getting a sense of possibility, you eventually train yourself to see opportunities that most people are blind to.

They are all caught up in the moment. A lot of them let their emotions get the best of them. But here you are, seeing possibilities, and this can lead you to better outcomes.

Why? You're exactly the kind of person people would want to talk to. Where everybody sees a win-lose or even a lose-lose situation, you might be the person who might be able to craft together a win-win situation. All of a sudden, you become very popular.

A Sense of Adventure

A lot of people think that whenever they are faced with challenges that it's a grim time of trial. They get very somber, very serious. Some get very sad. Well, if your trigger normally provoked depression or a very sobering sense of seriousness, why not swap it out with a sense of adventure?

The problem with seeing challenges as a call to focused, quiet, heavy concentration is that it sucks out all the fun out of overcoming the challenge. You have to understand that challenges are simply puzzles. That's what they are.

And the reason why a lot of people love playing puzzle games, trivia games or strategy games is that there is a sense of adventure out there. There's a lot that's unknown, there are certain things that you do know, and you're basically left to connect the dots and make sense of what would otherwise be a chaotic and confusing situation.

A lot of people automatically run away from this, a lot of people shrink from this, but it's a very empowering feeling when your sense of adventure gets triggered. Instead of automatically shrinking back, you're the first one to roll up your sleeves and try something new.

Associate these mental and emotional states with your trigger. It's not going to be easy at first, but the more you do it, the more you can turn your situation around. Instead of certain triggers bringing out the very worst in you, allow those triggers to put you in a state of flow.

CHAPTER 9

CHANGE YOUR REALITY
THROUGH CHANGED ACTIONS

As I've mentioned previously, the world doesn't care about your feelings. All it cares about are the actions you take.

If you think about this, it makes all the sense in the world because most people are not mind readers. Also, the road to hell is paved with good intentions.

It doesn't really matter what's motivating you or how good your intentions are, people are looking for the end result. What did you actually do? This is the point when the chain of Mentalism bears fruit.

Previously, a lot of the action was happening in between your ears and in your heart. Now, these are very important, but let's get real here. All of life's rewards really boils down to what you do.

Can you do the job or not? Do you know your stuff or not? Can you produce results or not? That's the bottom line.

And there's very little lying here because it's a black and white situation, if you think about it. It's on or off. It's yes or no. It's very binary.

And unfortunately, people are too content to just coast through life thinking that since they failed in the past or were unhappy or unfulfilled in the past that that pattern will continue. They have basically just given up on themselves because they think that, regardless of how hard they try, regardless of the kind of changes they want to make, nothing seems to change as far as their actions are concerned.

78

The Secret to Actions

Believe it or not, your actions are habitual. You tend to make certain decisions because of how you habitually interpret your stimuli and your emotional states. These flow from habits. They all involve triggers, habitual mental action, and rewards.

While it may seem automatic at this point, they were still chosen. The fact that they became a habit now is because you kept choosing them in the past. You chose them initially, and you kept repeating them.

Now, they seem automatic. In fact, they might seem that they are just part of who you are or are hardwired into your personality. You might even think that they are unchanging or that they're just so integral to who you are as a person.

But these are just excuses you give yourself because, believe it or not, you're more changeable than you give yourself credit for. You can change if you really want to. And while I understand that, in the action part of the mentalist sequence it is very difficult to change directions, it can still be done.

Ideally, you should change the mindset part because that's where you have the most control. That's the part that has less moving parts. When you try to change your habits at the action level, it's like trying to stop a freight train after it has picked up speed. Not exactly impossible, but not easy either.

Again, I want you to wrap your mind around the empowering truth that your actions, no matter how seemingly hardwired and automatic they may be, are habitual because you chose them early on. Focus on your ability to choose.

Change Your Habitual Actions and You Change Your Life

Let's put it this way, if you're struggling with money, it's because you have certain financial habits. You spend more than you earn. Do you put everything on your credit card?

Do you buy all sorts of trinkets that you don't really need? You only have one person to blame, and that's yourself.

Now, instead of wallowing in self-pity or, worse yet, painting yourself out to be some sort of victim, change your habitual actions. Instead of automatically whipping out the plastic, you might want to eat out less. You might want to swap out expensive activities for activities that are free. Instead of going to the movies, you might want to go jogging or go to the park.

I know this sounds pretty mundane, it might even seem basic or common sense, but these are real. These may seem small, but these add up to changes in your habits and attitudes that changes your behavior for the better.

You have to create a disconnect between the emotional states you get and the physical habits you take. Either you change your desired emotional state, which leads to better actions, or you change your physical actions despite your emotional state. Whatever the case may be, something's gotta give.

You don't have to do the exact same stuff as before when you get triggered. You can choose to do something else.

The Secret to Success

Do you think highly successful people don't get angry? Do you think they don't get tempted sexually? Of course, they do. They're human beings like you and me. But what makes them successful is they act from integrity.

Integrity really means focusing on your values and your character and acting accordingly. Sure, it's very easy to just take this shortcut each and every time. It's easy to just duck out of every duty, responsibility and obligation you have. After all, as I've mentioned several times in this training, taking the path of least resistance is a key part of the human condition.

But successful people are successful precisely because they chose to act out from integrity. In other words, they selected the type of person they want to be in terms of values and character, and they let their physical options flow from that.

This means that they're no longer slaves to their circumstances. And no matter how the world slaps, spits or mistreats them, they find it in themselves to react with class, dignity and civility.

This is not always easy but understand that living with integrity is very much like working out at the gym. When you first hit the weights, your muscles hated you for it. It felt like murder. You were in so much pain.

But as you challenge your muscles, they got stronger and stronger until you reach a point where the weight setting that you're in has become easy, so you then scale up. Maybe you add ten pounds or twenty pounds, and the process repeats itself again. Every time you scale up though, it hurts less and less. You adjust faster and faster.

The same applies to success. Living with integrity is going to seem very strange at first. You would feel like you're some sort of fish out of water. But the more you keep it up, the more you become the character you have focused on.

Remember, success is a choice-but it is rooted in habits.

CONCLUSION

The mentalist life is not an easy one. However, if you want a life of possibility and power, it is the life for you.

The best part to Mentalism is that you don't need a special machine. You don't need drugs. You don't need expensive therapists.

You don't need to go on some sort of long, mystical journey. Instead, you go on a journey within yourself and you focus on your inner reality.

By working with this inner reality instead of making excuses for it and getting terrified by it or sweeping it under the rug, Mentalism enables you to live a more empowered life. Whatever difficulties and struggles you currently have can be solved by claiming your power to choose.

I wish you nothing but the greatest contentment, happiness and fulfillment.

Printed by Libri Plureos GmbH in Hamburg, Germany